Crochet Bag Tutorials

Bags Crochet Patterns

Copyright © 2023

All rights reserved.

DEDICATION

The author and publisher have provided this e-book to you for your personal use only. You may not make this e-book publicly available in any way. Copyright infringement is against the law. If you believe the copy of this e-book you are reading infringes on the author's copyright, please notify the publisher at: https://us.macmillan.com/piracy

Crochet Bag Tutorials

Contents

Trendy Crochet Bag Pattern 1

Crochet Market Bag DIY 15

BOHO TASSEL CROCHET BAG 26

Crochet Cross Body Bag 44

CHOCOLATE TOTE 55

Trendy Crochet Bag Pattern

Show off your crochet skills and stay on trend when you make a crocheted circle bag! This free pattern for a crossbody purse uses thick rope as a base to form coiled sides covered with single crochet. The edges and strap stretch just enough to make this comfortable to wear while also holding all your essentials.

If you've never crocheted around rope before, it feels different than standard crochet, and you'll need to get used to the tension. To keep the stitches close (so nothing slips out of the bag), the suggested hook is smaller than usual. These factors do mean that at times, the crochet is a workout. But it's still easy enough for crocheters who

Crochet Bag Tutorials

know the basics of crochet.

Crossbody Circle Purse Project Information

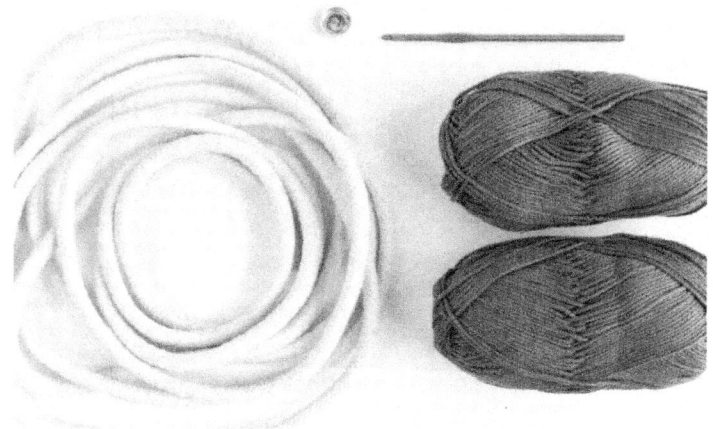

Project Level

Easy to Intermediate

Supplies

10 yards of 9mm braided cotton tope

2 skeins of Lion Brand 24/7 cotton yarn in Cafe Au Lait or approximately 300 yards of medium-weight cotton yarn

Crochet Bag Tutorials

Shank-back button

Tools

Size I/9 5.5mm crochet hook

Needle and thread

Large tapestry needle

Gauge

Gauge is not vital in this project.

Prepare the Rope

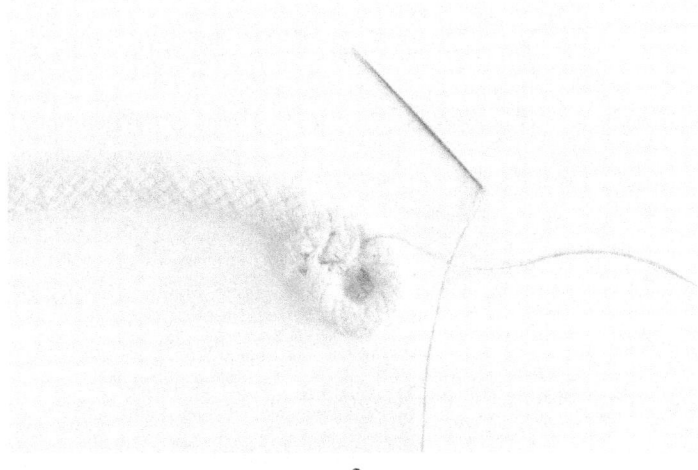

Crochet Bag Tutorials

Cut the rope in half so you have two five-yard pieces. Curl one end of a piece of rope to make a small ring. Use a sewing needle and matching thread to sew the rope ring in place.

Attach the Yarn to the Rope

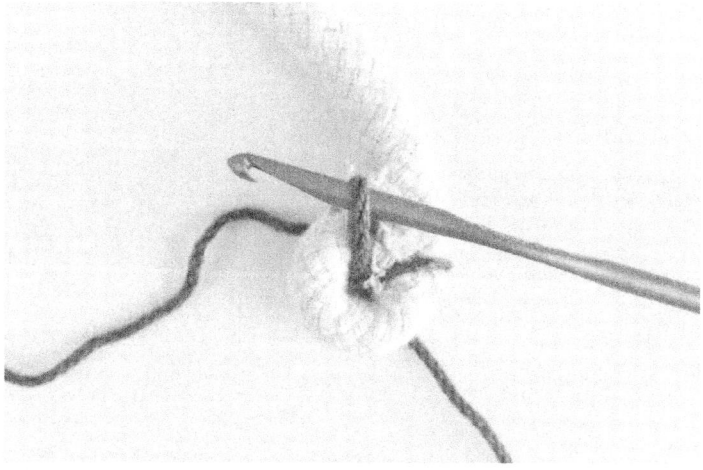

Hold the rope so it coils toward the left. Tie the yarn to the rope and draw up a loop through the center of the rope.

Begin Crocheting Around the Rope

Crochet Bag Tutorials

Round 1: Starting at the joined point of the rope ring, single crochet 9 stitches around the rope.

Round 2: Working around the rope, single crochet 3 stitches into the first stitch from round 1. Single crochet 2 stitches in each remaining stitch.

Attach a small safety pin as a marker for the end of the round. Move the marker up with each new round.

Continue Crocheting the Coiled Piece

Crochet Bag Tutorials

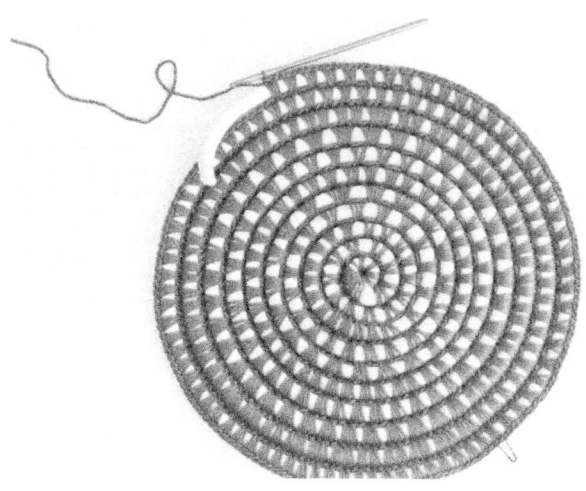

Round 3: Single crochet 2 stitches in every stitch.

Round 4: *Single crochet 2 in the space between the groupings of 2 stitches from the previous round, chain 1 and skip a stitch. Repeat from *.

Round 5: Single crochet 3 in every chain-space.

Round 6: *Skip 1 stitch, single crochet 2 in the next stitch, single crochet 2 in the space between the groupings of stitches from the previous round. Repeat from *.

Crochet Bag Tutorials

Rounds 7 & 8: Single crochet 2 in every space between the groupings of stitches from the previous round.

Round 9: Single crochet 3 in every space between the groupings of stitches from the previous round.

Round 10: Skip 1 stitch, single crochet 2 in the space between the groupings of stitches from the previous round, single crochet 2 in the next stitch. Repeat from *.

Round 11: Single crochet 2 in every space between the groupings of stitches from the previous round. Repeat to the end of the rope.

Finish the Crochet on the Rope

Crochet Bag Tutorials

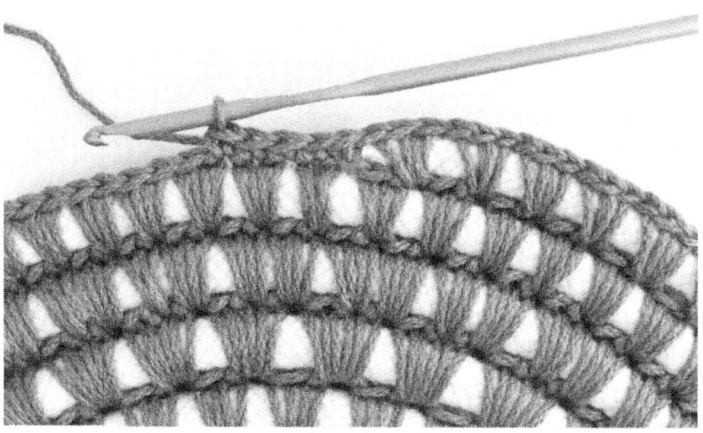

When the rope ends, work stitches over the end of the rope as much as possible, pushing the very end to the back of your crochet.

Work 10 single crochet stitches into the stitches from the previous round. End off the yarn.

Weave in all the ends. Make a second coiled piece to match the first.

Make the Strap and Purse Sides

Crochet Bag Tutorials

Note: Chain 3s at the beginning of each row does not count as a stitch. Make the first double crochet in the first stitch of the row.

Chain 15.

Row 1: Starting in the 3rd chain from the hook, work 12 double crochets.

Row 2: Chain 3, double crochet 12 stitches. Turn.

Repeat row 2 a total of 42 times.

Crochet Bag Tutorials

Row 3: Chain 3, double crochet 2 together, double crochet 8, double crochet 2 together. Turn.

Row 4: Chain 3, double crochet 2 together, double crochet 6, double crochet 2 together. Turn.

Row 5: Chain 3, double crochet 8 stitches. Turn.

Repeat row 5 a total of 75 times.

Row 6: Chain 3, double crochet 2 stitches into the first stitch, double crochet 6, double crochet 2 stitches into the last stitch. Turn.

Row 7: Chain 3, double crochet 2 stitches into the first stitch, double crochet 8, double crochet 2 stitches into the last stitch. Turn.

End off the yarn.

Slip stitch the two ends together and weave in all the ends.

Attach the Strap and Sides

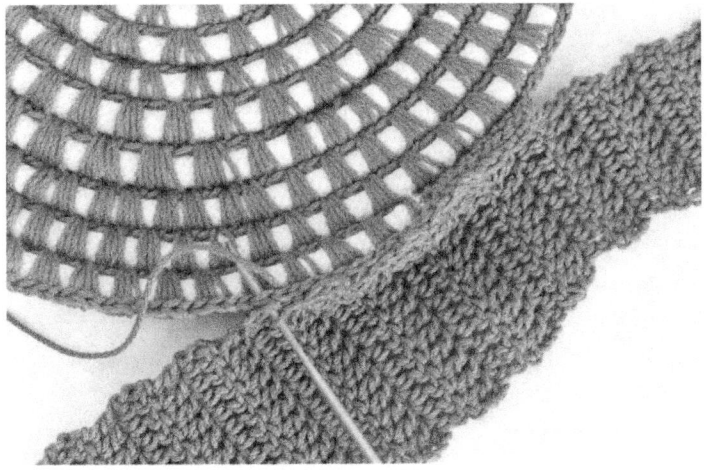

With the wrong sides together, hold a coiled piece with the side/strap piece. Align the point where the strap goes from wide to narrow with the last 10 single crochet stitches on the coiled side.

Use slip stitch to join the wide part of the crocheted band to the coiled side. Stop when the band narrows again.

Crochet Bag Tutorials

Repeat on the other side of the bag. Weave in all the yarn ends.

Make the Button Closure

Use yarn to sew a shank-style button centered on the top of one side of the purse. Stitch the button in place through the stitches in the coils.

Join yarn to the back of the purse in the same position as the button. Chain 20, then end off the yarn. Attach the end of the chain to the purse at the starting position to form a loop.

Note: This loop needs to be able to fit over the button to hold the bag closed, If you are using a large button, you make need to add more chains to the loop. Before securing the end, hold or pin the end to ensure that the loop is long enough.

Weave in the yarn ends.

Crochet Circle Bag Tips and Ideas

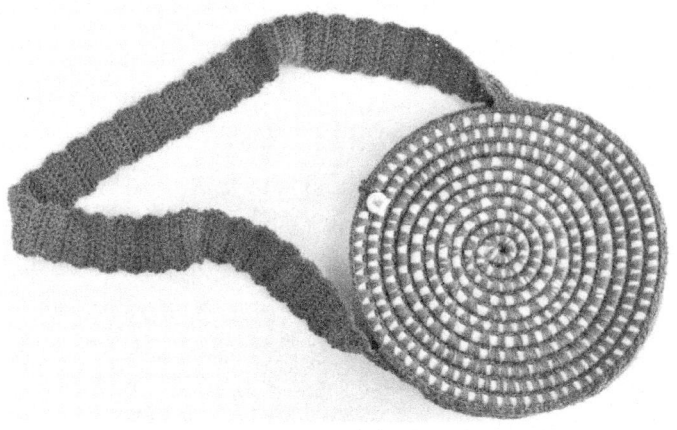

Try these tips and ideas when planning and making your project!

Avoid the need for changing yarn mid-coil by starting a new skein for the second half of the bag. It's easier to attach more yarn when making the strap piece.

Crochet Bag Tutorials

Although this is written with specific stitch patterns, you may find that you need to adjust the clusters of stitches as you work around the coils depending on your rope and yarn. The goal is to make circles that lie flat.

Want a bigger or smaller purse? Start with more or less rope and follow the pattern as closely as possible, adjusting as needed.

For a fun pop of color, use a contrasting yarn color when you attach the strap/sides to the coiled pieces. It will look like piping!

If you use variegated yarn, you'll get a fun effect on the coils.

Have fun and enjoy the process!

Crochet Market Bag DIY

Carry your shopping and other essentials in style in this easy and fun to crochet market bag. The free pattern is simple enough to complete in a weekend and perfect for trips to the farmer's market or the beach.

The rounds of open crochet have short and long chain-space gaps, resembling written Morse code. And while it doesn't spell anything, it's still filled with the markings that make it a Dots and Dashes Market Bag.

The shape and the yarn give this tote lots of stretch, so if you find that it looks a little big for your needs, you can easily shorten the bag or strap.

Market Bag Project Information

Cotton Yarn and Crochet Hook for Market Bag

Easy to Intermediate

Materials

Yarn: 2 skeins of Lily Sugar'n Cream Big Ball yarn in Teal or approximately 365 yards of worsted-weight cotton yarn.

Crochet Bag Tutorials

Hook: I/9 5.5mm

Other Notions: large tapestry needle.

Gauge

Gauge is not vital in this project.

Abbreviations

ch = chain stitch

ch-sp = chain space

dc = double crochet

dc2tog = double crochet two together

rep = repeat

sk = skip

sl st = slip stitch

st(s) = stitch(es)

Crochet Bag Tutorials

Crochet the Bag Base

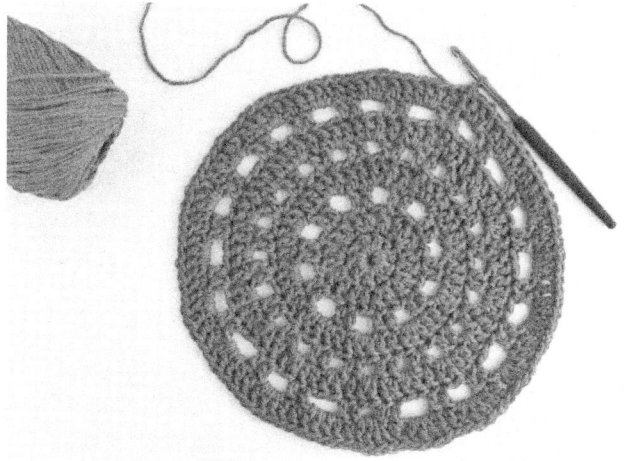

Ch 4. Sl st to join.

Round 1: Ch 3, dc 9 into the ring.

Round 2: Ch 3, dc in 1st st, ch 1. *2dc in next st, ch 1. Rep from * to end. Sl st to join.

Round 3: Ch 3, dc in 1st st, ch 2 and sk 1 st. *dc in next 2 sts, ch 2 and sk 1 st. Rep from * to end. Sl st to join.

Round 4: Ch 3, dc in 1st st, 3dc in ch-sp. *dc in next 2 sts, 3dc in ch-sp. Rep from * to end. Sl st to join.

Round 5: Ch 3, dc in 1st st, ch 1 and sk 1 st, [dc, ch 1, dc] in same st, ch 1 and sk 1 st. *dc in next 2 sts, ch 1 and sk 1 st, [dc, ch 1, dc] in same st, ch 1 and sk 1 st. Rep from * to end. Sl st to join.

Round 6: Ch 3, dc in 1st st, 2dc in ch-sp. *dc in next 2 sts, 2dc in ch-sp. Rep from * to end. Sl st to join.

Round 7: Ch 3, dc in 1st st, ch 2 and sk 2 sts, dc in next 2 sts, ch 2 and sk 1 st. *dc in next 2 sts, ch 2 and sk 2 sts, dc in next 2 sts, ch 2 and sk 1 st. Rep from * to end. Sl st to join.

Round 8: Ch 3, dc in 1st st, 3dc in ch-sp. *dc in next 2 sts, 3dc in ch-sp. Rep from * to end. Sl st to join.

Round 9: Ch 3, dc in 1st st, ch 1 and sk 1 st, [dc, ch 1, dc] in same st, ch 1 and sk 1 st. *dc in next 2 sts, ch 1 and sk 1 st, [dc, ch 1, dc] in same st, ch 1 and sk 1 st. Rep from * to end. Sl st to join.

Round 10: Ch 3, dc in 1st st, 3dc in ch-sp. *dc in next 2 sts, 3dc in ch-sp. Rep from * to end. Sl st to join.

Crochet the Bag Sides

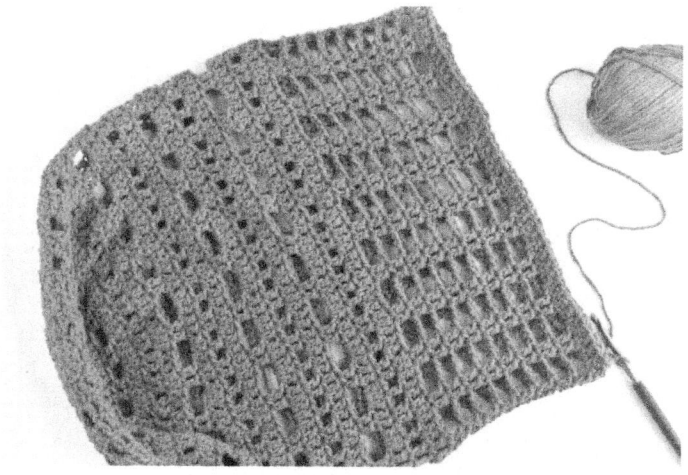

Round 11: Ch 3, dc in 1st st, ch 3 and sk 3 sts. *dc in next 2 sts, ch 3 and sk 3 sts. Rep from * to end. Sl st to join.

Round 12: Ch 3, dc in 1st st, 3dc in ch-sp. *dc in next 2 sts, 3dc in ch-sp. Rep from * to end. Sl st to join.

Round 13: Ch 3, dc in 1st st, ch 1 and sk 1 st, dc, ch 1 and sk 1 st. *dc in next 2 sts, ch 1 and sk 1 st, dc, ch 1 and sk 1 st. Rep from * to end. Sl st to join.

Round 14: Ch 3, dc in every st and ch-sp. Sl st to join.

Repeat rounds 11-14 two times more (12 rounds total).

Repeat round 11 eight times more.

Note: This makes a tall market bag, but if you want to make yours shorter, you can eliminate one repeat of rounds 11-14 and/or several repeats of round 11.

Round 15: Ch 3, dc in 1st st, 2dc in ch-sp. *dc in next 2 sts, 2dc in ch-sp. Rep from * to end. Sl st to join.

Crochet Bag Tutorials

Make the Straps

With yarn still attached, sl stitch 8 to work over to the starting point for the first strap.

Row 1: Ch 2, dc 16, turn.

Row 2: Ch 2, dc2tog, dc to last 2 sts, dc2tog, turn.

Repeat row 2 three times more (8 sts remain).

Row 3: Ch 2, dc 8, turn.

Repeat row 3 twelve times more, end off.

Make the Second Strap

Count 23 sts over from the edge of the first strap and join yarn.

Repeat rows 1-3 as described above. The strap should be centered on the opposite side of the first strap.

Finish the Market Bag

Crochet Bag Tutorials

Hold the ends of the strap pieces with right sides together and join them with slip stitch.

Weave in all ends on the bag.

Head to the Market

Keep your finished bag with you for when you need a reusable shopping bag or carry your towel and sunscreen with you to the beach!

If you want to use this as a purse, you can also sew a simple liner with

Crochet Bag Tutorials

a round bottom and stitch it in place so nothing falls through the dots and dashes.

BOHO TASSEL CROCHET BAG

Is it warming up in your part of the world yet? It's definitely been feeling summery here in the desert for a while now, and I was ready to bust out my cotton for some warm weather crochet. I was at Target recently (when is that statement ever NOT true?), and I saw this cute little crocheted bag and decided to try to recreate it at home.

Crochet Bag Tutorials

Sure, you could totally just buy the Target bag for 30 bucks. Sure, I probably spent half that in supplies plus at least three hours making this bag. Sure, sure. But that's not really the point, is it? The point is that I MADE this thing, and I am dang proud of that. I mean, it's so cute, right?

HERE'S WHAT YOU NEED TO MAKE YOUR OWN BOHO TASSEL BAG:

Worsted Weight Cotton Yarn (I used about 8 ounces of Lily Sugar N Cream in Ecru)

Size I (5.5 mm) Crochet Hook

Half a Yard of Unbleached Muslin

2 Steel Rings

Rivets and Rivet Setter

Leather Strip or an old belt would work great too.

Leather Punch

This pattern is written using American crochet terms.

Crochet Bag Tutorials

Special Stitches

Half Treble Crochet (htrc) – Yarn over twice, insert hook into work, yarn over (four loops on hook), yarn over and draw through two loops (three loops on hook), yarn over and draw through all loops.

Bag Front

Round 1: Starting with a magic loop, ch 2 (counts as first dc), work 11 dc in magic loop, pull to tighten, sl st to join (12 dc).

Crochet Bag Tutorials

Round 2: Ch 3 (counts as first dc and ch 1), dc , ch 1 in each stitch around, sl st to join (12 dc, 12 ch 1 sps).

Round 3: Ch 2 (counts as first dc), 2 dc in next ch 1 sp, *dc in next dc, 2 dc in next ch 1 sp, repeat from * around, sl st to top of first ch 2 to join (36 dc).

Round 4: Ch 4 (counts as first dc and ch 2), skip 1 dc, dc in next st, *ch 2, skip 1 dc, dc in next st, repeat from * around, sl st to 2nd ch of beginning ch 4 (18 dc, 18 ch 2 spaces).

Round 5: Ch 2 (counts as first dc), 2 dc in ch 2 sp, *dc in next st, 2 dc in next ch 2 sp, repeat from * around sl st to first ch 2 (54 dc).

Round 6: Ch 4 (counts as first dc and ch 2), skip 1 dc, dc in next st, *ch 2, skip 1 dc, dc in next st, repeat from * around sl st to 2 ch of beginning (27 dc, 27 ch 2 spaces).

Round 7: Ch 3 (counts as first htrc), (trc, htrc, htrc) all in next ch 2 sp, *dc in next dc, 2 dc in next ch 2 sp, repeat from * 18 times, dc in next st, (dc, htrc) in next ch 2 sp, htrc in next st, (trc, htrc, htrc) all in next ch 2 sp, dc in next dc, 2 dc in next ch 2 sp, hdc in next st, 2 hdc in next ch 2 sp, sc in next st, 2 sc in next ch 2 sp, sc in next st, 2 hdc in next ch 2 sp, hdc in next st, 2 dc in next ch 2 sp, sl st to beginning ch 3 to join. Weave off, finish in ends.

Bag Back

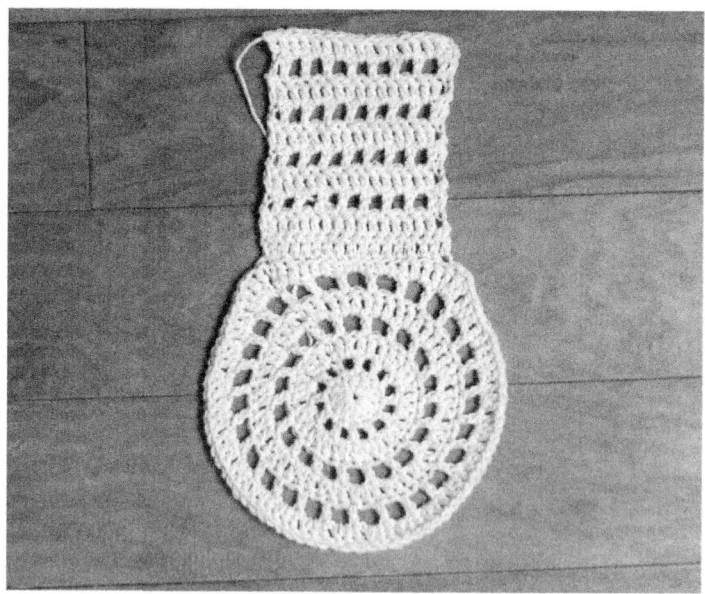

Crochet Bag Tutorials

The back of the bag is worked the same as the front but with a flap added to the top.

Round 1: Starting with a magic loop, ch 2 (counts as first dc), work 11 dc in magic loop, pull to tighten, sl st to join (12 dc).

Round 2: Ch 3 (counts as first dc and ch 1), dc , ch 1 in each stitch around, sl st to join (12 dc, 12 ch 1 sps).

Round 3: Ch 2 (counts as first dc), 2 dc in next ch 1 sp, *dc in next dc, 2 dc in next ch 1 sp, repeat from * around, sl st to top of first ch 2 to join (36 dc).

Round 4: Ch 4 (counts as first dc and ch 2), skip 1 dc, dc in next st, *ch 2, skip 1 dc, dc in next st, repeat from * around, sl st to 2nd ch of beginning ch 4 (18 dc, 18 ch 2 spaces).

Round 5: Ch 2 (counts as first dc), 2 dc in ch 2 sp, *dc in next st, 2 dc in next ch 2 sp, repeat from * around sl st to first ch 2 (54 dc).

Crochet Bag Tutorials

Round 6: Ch 4 (counts as first dc and ch 2), skip 1 dc, dc in next st, *ch 2, skip 1 dc, dc in next st, repeat from * around sl st to 2 ch of beginning (27 dc, 27 ch 2 spaces).

Round 7: Ch 3 (counts as first htrc), (trc, htrc, htrc) all in next ch 2 sp, *dc in next dc, 2 dc in next ch 2 sp, repeat from * 18 times, dc in next st, (dc, htrc) in next ch 2 sp, htrc in next st, (trc, htrc, htrc) all in next ch 2 sp, dc in next dc, 2 dc in next ch 2 sp, hdc in next st, 2 hdc in next ch 2 sp, sc in next st, 2 sc in next ch 2 sp, sc in next st, 2 hdc in next ch 2 sp, hdc in next st, 2 dc in next ch 2 sp, sl st to beginning ch 3 to join. Ch 2 (counts as first dc), TURN.

Now the pattern will switch from rounds to rows.

Row 1: Ch 2 (counts as first dc), working in back loops only, dc in each of next 16 sts (17 dc total). Turn.

Crochet Bag Tutorials

Row 2: Ch 2 (counts as first dc), dc in next st and each st across (17 dc). Turn.

Row 3: Ch 2 (counts as first dc), dc in next st, *ch 1, dc in next st, repeat from * six times, dc in next st (10 dcs, 7 ch 1 sps). Turn.

Row 4: Ch 2 (counts as first dc), dc in next st and each st across (17 dc). Turn.

Row 5: Ch 2 (counts as first dc), dc in next st, *ch 1, dc in next st, repeat from * six times, dc in next st (10 dcs, 7 ch 1 sps). Turn.

Row 6: Ch 2 (counts as first dc), dc in next st and each st across (17 dc). Turn.

Row 7: Ch 2 (counts as first dc), dc in next st, *ch 1, dc in next st, repeat from * six times, dc in next st (10 dcs, 7 ch 1 sps). Turn.

Row 8: Ch 2 (counts as first dc), dc in next st and each st across (17

Crochet Bag Tutorials

dc). Turn.

Row 9: Ch 2 (counts as first dc), Turn dc in next st, *ch 1, dc in next st, repeat from * six times, dc in next st (10 dcs, 7 ch 1 sps). Turn.

Row 10: Ch 2 (counts as first dc), dc in next st and each st across (17 dc). Finish off, weave in ends.

Bag Side Panel

Row 1: Ch 8, dc in 3rd ch from hook, dc in remaining 5 chs (6 dc total). Turn.

Row 2: Ch 2 (counts as first dc), dc in each of next 5 sts (6 dc total). Turn.

Repeat Row 2 until the piece is long enough to wrap around the outside of the bag front — about 37 rows.

To join the front of the bag to the side panel, hold the wrong sides together and work single crochets through both layers.

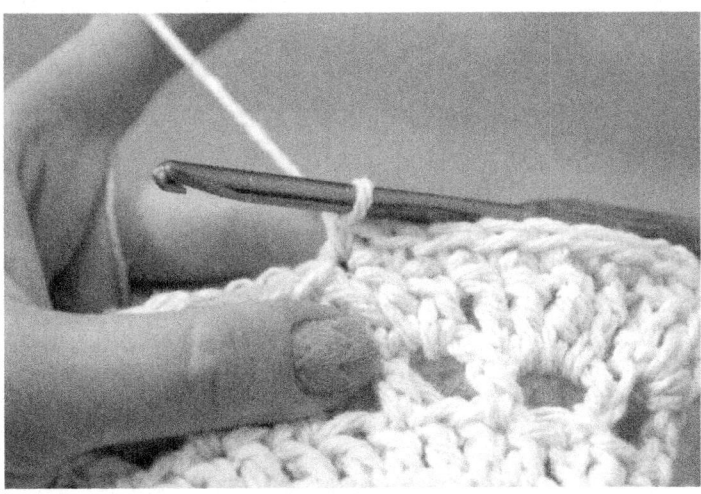

Crochet Bag Tutorials

When the pieces are all joined together, work a shell stitch edge around the outside seam you just made. Starting in the corner of sc seam of the front of the bag, ch 1 and single crochet in the same stitch. Skip two stitches and then work 5 dc into the next stitch. Skip two stitches and single crochet in the next stitch. Repeat this pattern (sc, skip 2 sts, 5 dc, skip w sts, sc) to form shells all around the outside of the front.

Work the shell stitch edge around the seam of the back of the bag as well, but continue to work the shell pattern around the flap as well. I worked three shells on each side of the flap.

Crochet Bag Tutorials

Your bag is all crocheted at this point! All that is left to do is add lining and straps.

To make the lining of the bag, use the bag as a guide and cut pattern pieces. You will need a front and back piece (you do not need to line the flap, so they should be the same shape and size) as well as a side panel piece.

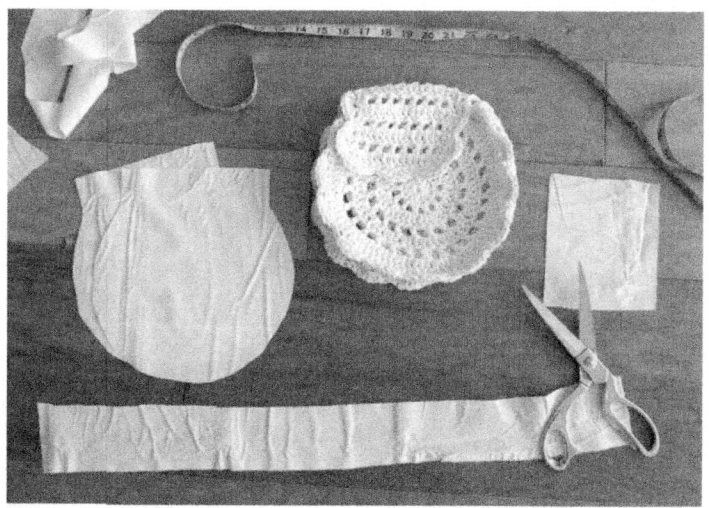

I added an extra inch or so to the top of the front and back piece patterns so I could turn it under to finish that opening. I also added a pocket to one of the pieces.

Crochet Bag Tutorials

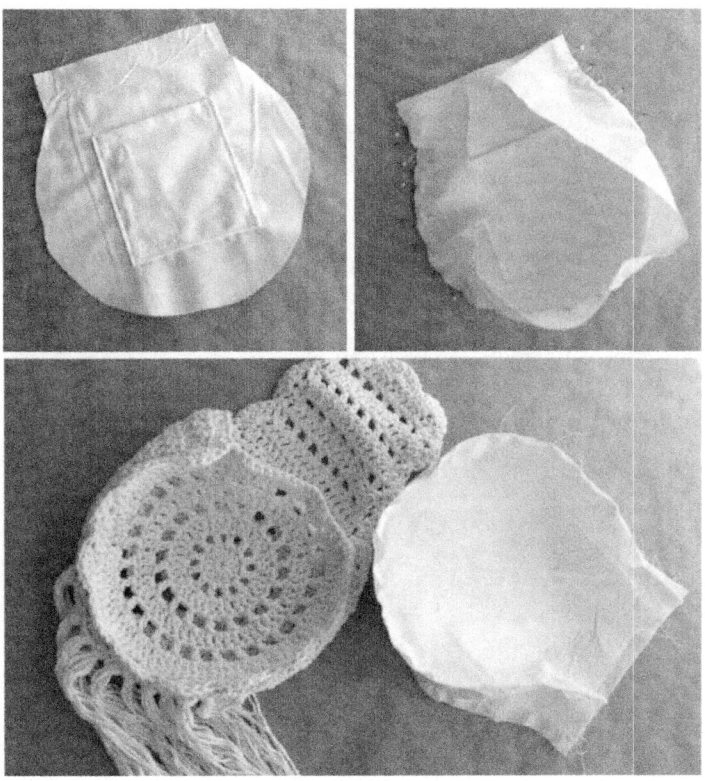

Pin the back or front piece to the side panel piece, and sew around the seam. Then repeat on the other side. Finally, stuff the lining into your crocheted bag and hand sew the lining into the bag.

Crochet Bag Tutorials

When the lining is sewn in, it's time to add the tassels! Cut five lengths of yarn, then fold them in half and use a large crochet hook to loop it around stitches along the bottom of the bag as well as the bottom of the flap.

Crochet Bag Tutorials

Finally, trim all of the tassels to the same length. I cut mine to 11 inches each.

Crochet Bag Tutorials

Last but not least, it's time to add a strap. You could crochet a strap, but I liked the contrast of the leather, and it was a good opportunity to work with a material I don't use all that often.

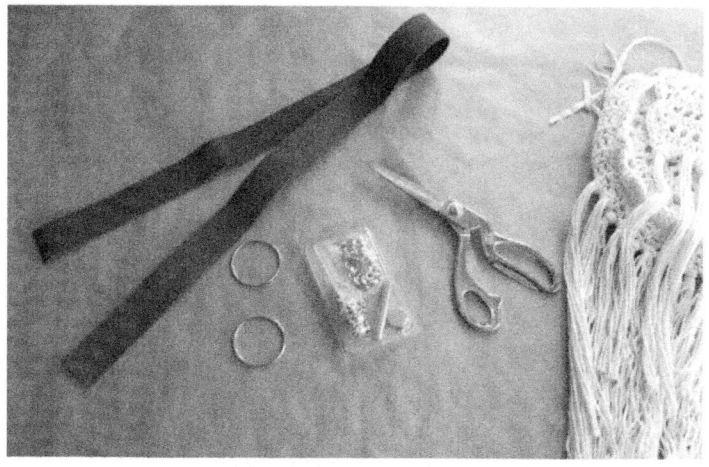

I started by cutting small pieces about an inch and a half long that I looped around the steel ring and attached to the bag using rivets.

To set the rivets, first punch a hole the right diameter for your rivets through the leather, then push the rivet through all layers, push the end on with your fingers, and then set the rivet with the setter and a hammer.

Crochet Bag Tutorials

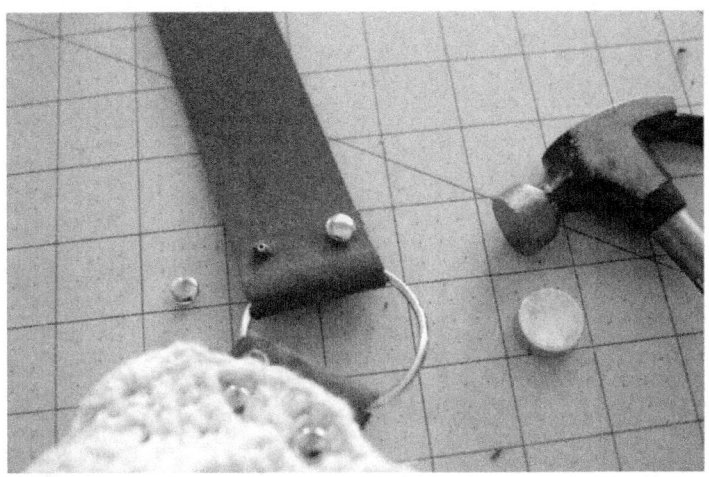

I repeated the process to join the strap to the rings. And that's it! My fun new summery bag was all done!

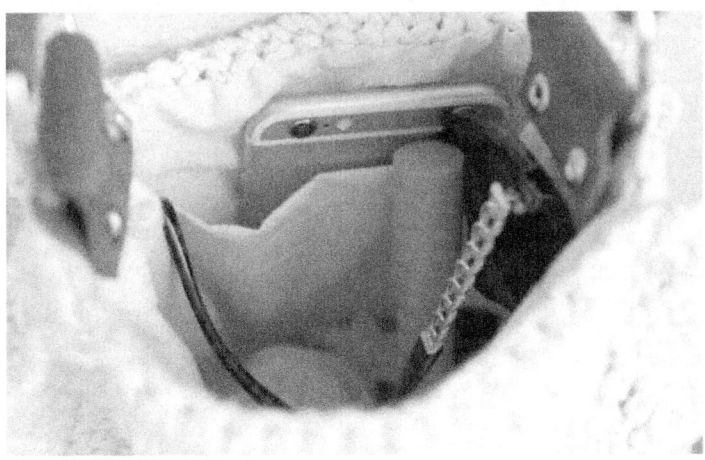

Crochet Cross Body Bag

Do you ever spot a chic crochet bag in a shop and think you can make it yourself? This pattern will help you create your own stylish

Crochet Bag Tutorials

cross body bag that is just as cute and functional as options you see in stores. You may have thought handmade crochet bags were all casual and stretchy, but this sturdy Crochet Cross Body Bag is an elegant take on a crochet purse pattern. This crossbody bag is crocheted using nylon for extra durability, and the optional jeweled tassel cap adds an extra touch of glamour.

Intermediate

Crochet HookF/5 or 3.75 mm hook

Yarn Weight(0) Lace (33-40 stitches to 4 inches). Includes crochet thread.

Crochet Gauge17 sts = 4" [10 cm]; 20 rows = 4" [10 cm] in single crochet (sc). CHECK YOUR GAUGE. Use any size hook to obtain the gauge.

Finished SizeBag measures about 10" [25.5 cm] wide, 9" [23 cm] high and 2½" [6.5 cm] deep, not including strap.

NOTES

Crochet Bag Tutorials

Bag is made in 5 pieces: Front, back, "sides" panel, flap and strap.

All pieces are worked separately then crocheted together with reverse single crochet.

The flap is embellished with a thick surface slip stitch curve and a tassel.

Use a drop of clear nail polish or super glue on all cut ends of nylon to ensure that weaved-in ends are secured.

A lining is suggested but not mandatory. Craft felt makes an easy-to-use, non-fraying alternative to traditional lining materials. Plastic canvas, especially placed inside the bag's bottom section, serves as support for the bag.

Decorative tassel caps can be found in the notions section of fabric and craft stores. Many purchased faux-leather tassels at local discount stores are constructed without glue. Try pulling out the faux-leather part and reusing the tassel cap.

SPECIAL STITCHES

reverse sc (reverse single crochet) = Work single crochet in opposite direction from which you would usually work (left to right if you are righthanded, and right to left if you are lefthanded). This stitch is also known as crab stitch. It creates a rope-like twisted single crochet edging.

sc2tog (single crochet 2 stitches together) = [Insert hook in next stitch, yarn over and pull up a loop] twice, yarn over and draw through all 3 loops on hook.

SPECIAL TECHNIQUES

Adjustable-ring = Wrap yarn into a ring, ensuring that the tail falls behind the working yarn. Grip ring and tail between middle finger and thumb. Insert hook through center of ring, yarn over (with working yarn) and draw up a loop. Work stitches of first round in the ring. After the first round of stitches is worked, pull gently on tail to tighten ring.

surface slip stitch = Make a slip knot and hold it on wrong side of piece, insert hook from right side to wrong side in space between stitches, place slip knot on hook and draw up loop (stretching the loop to about ½" [1.5 cm] long), *insert hook from right side to wrong side in next space, yarn over and draw loop through crochet

Crochet Bag Tutorials

fabric and through loop on hook; repeat from * as desired. To finish last surface slip stitch, on right side of piece, remove loop from hook, insert hook from wrong side to right side in next space, return loop to hook and draw it to the wrong side. Cut nylon, draw end through loop and pull to tighten. Weave in end securely.

ABBREVIATIONS

ch = chain; sc = single crochet; st(s) = stitch(es); [ ] = work directions in brackets the number of times specified.

FRONT

Beginning at top edge, ch 41.

Row 1: Sc in 2nd ch from hook and in each remaining ch across—40 sc.

Rows 2–34: Ch 1, turn, sc in each st across.

Shape Lower Section

Rows 35–42: Ch 1, turn, sc2tog, sc in each st to last 2 sts, sc2tog—24 sc remain in Row 42.

Fasten off.

BACK

Make same as front.

Crochet Bag Tutorials

FLAP

Beginning at center of top edge, make an adjustable ring. Work back and forth in rows (not rounds).

Row 1: Ch 1, 3 sc in ring.

Row 2: Ch 1, turn, 2 sc in each st across—6 sc.

Row 3: Ch 1, turn, 2 sc in first st, sc in next st, [2 sc in next st, sc in next st] twice—9 sc.

Row 4: Ch 1, turn, 2 sc in first st, sc in next 2 sts, [2 sc in next st, sc in next 2 sts] twice—12 sc.

Row 5: Ch 1, turn, 2 sc in first st, sc in next 3 sts, [2 sc in next st, sc in next 3 sts] twice—15 sc.

Row 6: Ch 1, turn, 2 sc in first st, sc in next 4 sts, [2 sc in next st, sc in next 4 sts] twice—18 sc.

Row 7: Ch 1, turn, 2 sc in first st, sc in next 5 sts, [2 sc in next st, sc in next 5 sts] twice—21 sc.

Row 8: Ch 1, turn, 2 sc in first st, sc in next 6 sts, [2 sc in next st, sc in next 6 sts] twice—24 sc.

Row 9: Ch 1, turn, 2 sc in first st, sc in next 7 sts, [2 sc in next st, sc in next 7 sts] twice—27 sc.

Row 10: Ch 1, turn, 2 sc in first st, sc in next 8 sts, [2 sc in next st, sc in next 8 sts] twice—30 sc.

Row 11: Ch 1, turn, 2 sc in first st, sc in next 9 sts, [2 sc in next st, sc in next 9 sts] twice—33 sc.

Row 12: Ch 1, turn, 2 sc in first st, sc in next 10 sts, [2 sc in next st, sc in next 10 sts] twice—36 sc.

Row 13: Ch 1, turn, 2 sc in first st, sc in next 11 sts, [2 sc in next st, sc in next 11 sts] twice—39 sc.

Row 14: Ch 1, turn, 2 sc in first st, sc in next 12 sts, [2 sc in next st, sc in next 12 sts] twice—42 sc.

Row 15: Ch 1, turn, 2 sc in first st, sc in next 13 sts, [2 sc in next st, sc in next 13 sts] twice—45 sc.

Row 16: Ch 1, turn, 2 sc in first st, sc in next 14 sts, [2 sc in next st, sc in next 14 sts] twice—48 sc.

Row 17: Ch 1, turn, 2 sc in first st, sc in next 15 sts, [2 sc in next st, sc in next 15 sts] twice—51 sc.

Row 18: Ch 1, turn, 2 sc in first st, sc in next 16 sts, [2 sc in next st, sc in next 16 sts] twice—54 sc.

Crochet Bag Tutorials

Row 19: Ch 1, turn, 2 sc in first st, sc in next 17 sts, [2 sc in next st, sc in next 17 sts] twice—57 sc.

Row 20: Ch 1, turn, 2 sc in first st, sc in next 18 sts, [2 sc in next st, sc in next 18 sts] twice—60 sc.

Row 21: Ch 1, turn, 2 sc in first st, sc in next 19 sts, [2 sc in next st, sc in next 19 sts] twice—63 sc.

Work Along Straight Edge (Top) of Flap

Row 1: Ch 1, do not turn, working in ends of rows, draw up a loop in end of next 2 rows, yarn over and draw through all 3 loops on hook (sc2tog made), sc in end of next 18 rows, draw up a loop in end of next row, draw up a loop in center adjustable ring, yarn over and draw through all 3 loops on hook (sc2tog made), sc in end of next 19 rows, sc2tog (working in ends of last 2 rows)—40 sc.

Rows 2–8: Ch 1, turn, sc in each st across

Do not fasten off.

Connect Flap to Back

Hold flap and back with wrong sides (insides) together and stitches of top edges matching. Use Knit Klips™ to hold the pieces together.

With right side of flap facing you and working through both thicknesses, reverse sc in each st across top edges to connect flap to back; continuing around remaining edges of front, reverse sc evenly spaced along curved edges of flap.

Fasten off.

"SIDES" PANEL

Ch 12.

Row 1: Sc in 2nd ch from hook and in each remaining ch across—11 sc.

Rows 2–112: Ch 1, turn, sc in each st across.

Do not fasten off.

Measure the "sides" panel to ensure it will fit correctly around the side and lower edges of the back. Work additional rows or unravel rows if necessary.

Connect "Sides" Panel to Back

Place back on flat surface with wrong side (inside) facing up. Beginning at one top corner and ending at other top corner of back, arrange one long edge of "sides" panel along sides and lower edges of back, use Knit Klips™ evenly spaced to hold the pieces together.

Crochet Bag Tutorials

Working from the right side (outside) and working through both thicknesses, join yarn at one corner and work reverse sc evenly spaced all the way along the edges to join "sides" panel to back.

Connect "Sides" Panel to Front

Place front on flat surface with wrong side (inside) facing up. Arrange remaining long edge of "sides" panel around sides and lower edges of front, use Knit Klips™ evenly spaced to hold the pieces together.

Working from the right side (outside) and working through both thicknesses, join yarn at one corner and work reverse sc evenly spaced all the way along the edges to join "sides" panel to front.

FINISHING

Surface Slip Stitch Line

Holding 3 strands of nylon together and beginning and ending at top edge of flap, work a surface slip stitch curve along the spaces between stitches of Row 17.

Tassel

Using 10–11" [25.5–28 cm] piece of heavy cardboard or a thin book, wrap nylon thread around the cardboard (or book) 25 times. Cut a 12" [30.5 cm] piece of nylon thread for tying tassel top. Thread the

Crochet Bag Tutorials

12" [30.5 cm] piece under one end of the wraps and tie a strong knot. Place a few drops of super glue in the tassel cap and quickly insert the tassel top section into the cap. Once dried, trim the tassel to create a clean edge. Follow instructions on tassel cap package to attach tassel to bag flap.

Lining (Optional)

Line the bag if desired. Refer to the Notes on suggested methods and materials. Weave in any remaining ends.

CHOCOLATE TOTE

WHAT YOU'LL NEED:

Yarn: Deborah Norville Serenity Chunky, each approximately 109 yards/100m (acrylic): 4 balls #7036 Fudge

Hook: K (6.5 mm)

Notions: Yarn needle

    Handles

    Craft Stabilizer (optional)

    Lining Fabric (optional)

Crochet Bag Tutorials

Matching Thread (if needed for lining and handles)

SKILL LEVEL: Easy

FINISHED MEASUREMENTS: approximately 13" wide, 10" tall and 4 1/2" deep not including handles

GAUGE: 10 sts and 12 rows = 4"

Special Stitches:

Extra Extended Single Crochet (eesc): Insert hook into st and pull up a loop, (yo, pull through one loop on hook) twice, yo and pull through all loops on hook.

Pocket Lining (make two):

Ch 14.

Row 1: Sc in 2nd ch from hook and each ch across; turn – 13 sts.

Rows 2-14: Ch 1, work even in sc; turn.

Fasten off.

Front:

Ch 40.

Row 1: Sc in 2nd ch from hook and each ch across; turn – 39 sts.

Row 2: Ch 1, sc in next st, *eesc in next st, sc in next st; rep from * across; turn.

Row 3: Ch 1, work even in sc; turn.

Rows 4: Ch 1, sc in first 2 sts, *eesc in next st, sc in next st; rep from * across to last st, sc in last st; turn.

Row 5: Ch 1, work even in sc; turn.

Rows 6-13: Repeat rows 2-5.

Row 14: Repeat row 2.

Row 15: Ch 1, sc 13, sc across 13 sts of top of pocket lining, sk 13 sts of front, sc last 13 sts of front.

Rows 16-17: Repeat rows 4-5.

Rows 18-25: Repeat rows 2-5.

Rows 26-27: Repeat rows 2-3.

Fasten off.

Back:

Work same as front.

Side (make two):

Ch 14.

Row 1: Sc in 2nd ch from hook and each ch across – 13 sts.

Rows 2-17: Work even in sc.

Rows 18-25: Repeat rows 2-5 of front.

Rows 26-27: Repeat rows 2-3 of front.

Crochet Bag Tutorials

Fasten off.

Side Pocket (make two):

Ch 14.

Row 1: Sc in 2nd ch from hook and each ch across – 13 sts.

Rows 2-17: Repeat rows 2-5 of front.

Fasten off.

Bottom:

Ch 14.

Row 1: Sc in 2nd ch from hook and each ch across – 13 sts.

Rows 2-41: Repeat rows 2-5 of front.

Fasten off.

Finishing:

Sew side pocket on top of side at sides and bottom.

Sew pocket lining to front/back at sides and bottom.

Stitch front and back to sides.

Attach bottom.

Sew on handles.

Printed in Great Britain
by Amazon